# Wheels, wings and water

# Cars

## Chris Oxlade

**www.raintreepublishers.co.uk**
Visit our website to find out more information about **Raintree** books.

To order:
 Phone 44 (0) 1865 888112
Send a fax to 44 (0) 1865 314091
Visit the Raintree Bookshop at **www.raintreepublishers.co.uk** to browse our catalogue and order online.

First published in Great Britain by Raintree,
Halley Court, Jordan Hill, Oxford OX2 8EJ,
part of Harcourt Education.
Raintree is a registered trademark of Harcourt
Education Ltd.

Editorial: Charlotte Guillain and Isabel Thomas
Design: Sue Emerson (HL-US) and Joanna Sapwell
(www.tipani.co.uk)
Picture Research: Maria Joannou and
Su Alexander
Production: Lorraine Hicks

Originated by Dot Gradations
Printed and bound in China by South China
Printing Company

10 digit ISBN 1 844 21372 2 (hardback)
13 digit ISBN 978 1 844 21372 6 (hardback)
07 06 05 04 03
10 9 8 7 6 5 4 3 2 1

10 digit ISBN 1 844 21382 X (paperback)
13 digit ISBN 978 1 844 21382 5 (paperback)
08 07 06
10 9 8 7 6 5 4 3 2

**British Library Cataloguing in Publication Data**
Oxlade, Chris
Cars. – (Wheels, wings and water)
1.Automobiles – Juvenile literature
I.Title
388.3'42

**Acknowledgements**
The publishers would like to thank the following
for permission to reproduce photographs: action
plus, 16; Car Photo Library, 8, 22; Collections/ Andy
Hibbert, 14; Collections/ Joanna Lewis, 11;
Collections/ John Potts, 10; Corbis, 7, 15; Motoring
Picture Library, 12, 13 PA Photos, 19; Powerstock, 4;
Trip/ H Rogers, 6, 18, 21; Trip/ Mike Smith, 17; Trip/
Rover, 20; Trip/ Trip, 9; Tudor Photography, 5.

Cover photograph reproduced with permission of
Eye Ubiquitous

Every effort has been made to contact copyright
holders of any material reproduced in this book.
Any omissions will be rectified in subsequent
printings if notice is given to the publishers.

# Contents

What is a car? . . . . . . . . . . . . . . . . . 4

What kinds of car are there? . . . . . . . 6

What do car wheels do? . . . . . . . . . 8

What makes a car go? . . . . . . . . . . 10

How does a person drive a car? . . . . . 12

Where do cars go? . . . . . . . . . . . . . 14

How fast do cars go? . . . . . . . . . . . 16

What are racing cars? . . . . . . . . . . . 18

Where are cars made? . . . . . . . . . . 20

Car map . . . . . . . . . . . . . . . . . . 22

Glossary . . . . . . . . . . . . . . . . . . 23

Index . . . . . . . . . . . . . . . . . . . . 24

Some words are shown in bold, **like this**.
They are explained in the glossary on page 23.

# What is a car?

A car is a **vehicle** that carries people and things.

This family is going on holiday in their car.

These children have travelled to school by car.

People who travel in a car are called passengers.

# What kinds of car are there?

This tiny car is called a Smart car.

Small cars are good for driving in busy cities.

This very long car is called
a limousine.

There are big, soft seats in the back.

# What do car wheels do?

Cars have four wheels.

The wheels let the car roll along the road.

tyre

**Tyres** stop the wheels from slipping on the road.

They make the car ride less bumpy.

# What makes a car go?

A car has an **engine** that makes its wheels turn round.

When the wheels turn, the car moves along the road.

An engine needs **fuel** to make it work.

The fuel goes into the fuel tank at the back of the car.

# How does a person drive a car?

The driver steers the car with the **steering wheel**.

She presses pedals to speed up or slow down.

**Instruments** tell the driver if the car is working properly.

There is a switch to turn the **headlights** on and off.

# Where do cars go?

People drive their cars on roads and motorways.

This motorway is for driving fast.

Some cars can drive on muddy fields and across streams.

They are called off-road cars.

# What are racing cars?

Racing cars race each other on special tracks.

This is a Formula 1 racing car.

Rally cars race on bumpy, bendy tracks.

The fastest car wins the race.

# How fast do cars go?

This is a speedometer. It shows the driver how fast the car is going.

Most family cars can go up to 150 kilometres per hour.

This racing car is called a dragster.

It can go faster than 300 kilometres per hour.

# Where are cars made?

Cars are made in a big factory.

People add parts as the car moves through the factory.

Sometimes a car goes wrong.

The driver takes it to a garage to be mended.

# Car map

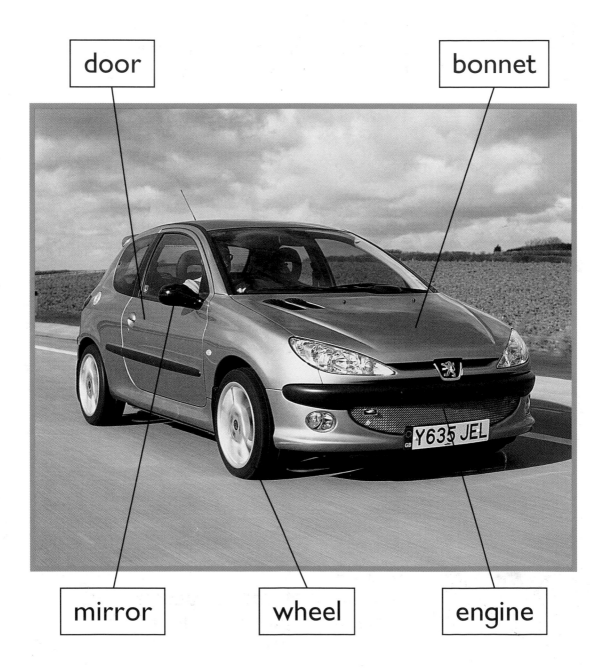

door

bonnet

mirror

wheel

engine

Y635 JEL

# Glossary

**engine**
machine that makes a vehicle move by making the wheels turn round

**fuel**
liquid or gas that burns in an engine to make energy

**headlights**
big lights at the front of a car to help the driver see the road at night

**instruments**
lights, dials and displays that show the driver how the car is working

**steering wheel**
wheel that the driver turns to make the car go left or right

**tyre**
thick, bumpy rubber strip on the outside of a wheel

**vehicle**
machine that carries people and things from place to place

# Index

bonnet  22

dragster  19

driver  12–13, 18

engine  10–11

factory  20

family car  4, 18

Formula 1 car  16

fuel  11

garage  21

headlights  13

instruments  13

limousine  7

mirror  22

motorway  14

off-road car  15

passenger  5

pedal  12

racing car  16, 19

rally car  17

road  8–10, 14

Smart car  6

speedometer  18

steering wheel  12

track  16–17

tyre  9

vehicle  4

wheel  8–10